CRUISE TO THE SOUTH SEA

Round Cape Horn on the Queen Mary 2

Hugh Leggatt

© Hugh Leggatt, 2016

Published by Leggatt

A CIP catalogue record for this book is available from the British Library.

ISBN 978-0-9955392-0-4

Photographs by Hugh Leggatt
Maps by Leo Hartas

Book layout and cover design by Clare Brayshaw

Prepared and printed by:

York Publishing Services Ltd
64 Hallfield Road
Layerthorpe
York YO31 7ZQ

Tel: 01904 431213

Website: www.yps-publishing.co.uk

Contents

First words   v

Ranch   1

Companions   9

Tierra del Fuego   17

Horn   25

Acknowledgements   36

About the author   37

Cover photograph: Cape Horn, the southernmost tip of South America, from the *Queen Mary 2*, February 2016.

First Words

Cape Horn, the southernmost point of South America, has a rather baleful reputation. It has been described as the uttermost part of the earth, desolate and wild, the abode of a terrible sea. It is nevertheless home to people of Argentina and Chile, it attracts intrepid round-the-world yachtsmen and -women, and also luxury tourists seeking to experience its famous storms and rough weather.

To go and see this bad boy cape in the comfort of the Cunard ocean liner, the *Queen Mary 2*, was an eye-catching prospect which I came across in March 2015, a year before departure. I decided it was an opportunity not to be missed, so signed up straight away to go to South America.

A visit to Tierra del Fuego and Cape Horn was part of the liner's 125-night world voyage in 2016. Every year the ship leaves Southampton in the middle of January and returns to England four months later in mid-May. The itinerary is different each year and does not often include Cape Horn. The Horn must have been a major drawcard as the ship was more or less sold out for the segment from east coast Rio de Janeiro, Brazil, to west coast Valparaiso, Chile.

Look at a map of the world, or the earth ball from space, and you see an awful lot of blue water along the bottom end. While the southern extremities of Africa, Australia and New Zealand poke into this watery void, it is the crooked finger at the end of South America, Cape Horn, that reaches the furthest south. And each side of this furthest cape is open water for the whole circumference of the globe except for small scraps of islands.

To the west of Cape Horn – the expanse that 16th and 17th century explorers called the South Sea and we call the Pacific Ocean – there is no land at all for nearly 6,000 miles to New Zealand. This is the direction the winds come from, the south-westerlies, blowing a continuous blast around the bottom of the world from west to east.

The absence of any obstruction over the face of these southern waters, unlike the almost continuous chain of land encircling the northern latitudes, helps explain the unpredictable violence of wind and sea conditions that make Cape Horn exposed and extreme. The winds across the southern oceans give these latitudes the names Roaring Forties, Furious Fifties and Screaming Sixties.

When a very difficult and arduous task has been accomplished, a person might sigh, "I've been round the Horn on this one", reflecting the Cape's uncompromising reputation. During the centuries before the Panama Canal opened in 1914, in order to get round the 8,500-mile-long barrier of the Americas, ships had to endure the hardships and dangers of stormy Cape Horn. The alternative was to go east round Africa's Cape of Good Hope and cross the Indian Ocean to Australia and the Pacific.

Magellan in 1520 was the first European to find a passage to the South Sea from the Atlantic. This was by way of Tierra del Fuego through the archipelago of hundreds of islands north of Cape Horn. In 1616 a Dutch merchant ship was blown off course south of Magellan's Strait and ended up discovering the true land's end, which they called *Kaap Hoorn* after their home port, Hoorn, in Holland. In Spanish it is *Cabo de Hornos*, the southernmost tip of Chile.

The great English circumnavigators Drake and Cavendish sailed through the Strait of Magellan in 1578 and 1587, the explorer and navigator James Cook visited the outer islands and Cape Horn in 1769 and again in 1774, and Charles Darwin was at Tierra del Fuego in 1832. These early voyages – especially to we moderns who have felt the chill winds and seen the gigantic waves of the austral summer – must have involved remarkable hardships.

But the 19th century clipper ships that plied their trade between Europe and the Pacific made the best of these conditions by sailing from the Atlantic east round Africa's Cape to Australia, and back to Europe round the Horn with the wind behind them all the way. This made them the fastest ships in the age of sail. But going round the Horn still meant plunging through mountainous seas in 80mph gales, and shipping water across the bows as the vessel pitched, heeled and rolled.

Not so on the *Queen Mary 2* which not only has fins that can be deployed from the hull to stabilise the ship, but can shoulder its way through the oncoming waves in the teeth of a Force 9 gale with all the assurance of a swan on a pond. She was built for the North Atlantic crossings from Southampton to New York and is at home in the Cape Horn weather.

This short book is not a day-by-day travelogue of life on board and the ports of call as was my 2012 account, *Cruise to Cape Town*, aboard the *QM2*. Rather it is a photographic record, with maps, and a description of four highlights of the voyage: a visit to a South American ranch; insights into life on board; an excursion on Tierra del Fuego; and impressions of Cape Horn itself, along with some maritime context.

There are places on earth you hear about that intrigue you. For me Cape Horn was one of them – remote, wild, dramatic and deadly. However, I must acknowledge that while the Horn came into my imagination as a lion, it went out like a lamb; meaning that the comforts of the 21st century have erased the terror and tamed the tempests. Drinking in the wild sights could be enjoyed from the deck of a luxurious liner with a glass of champagne in hand.

Hugh Leggatt

Farnham, March 2016

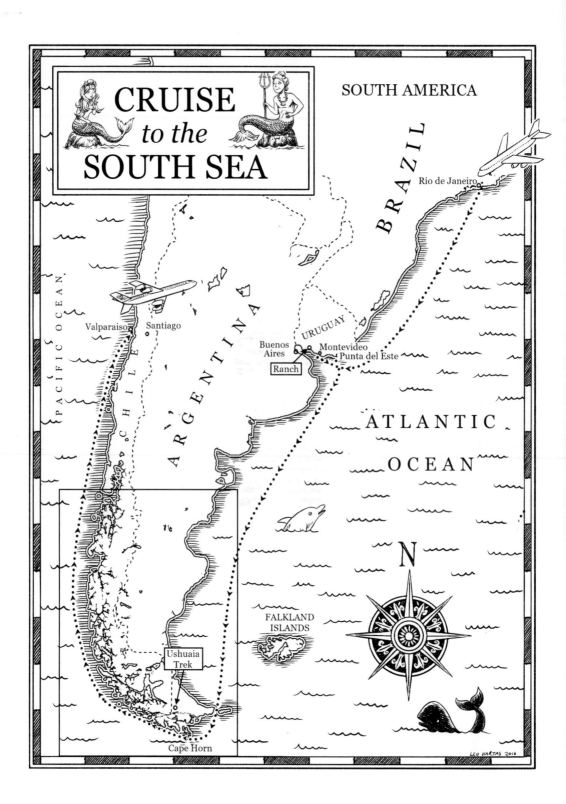

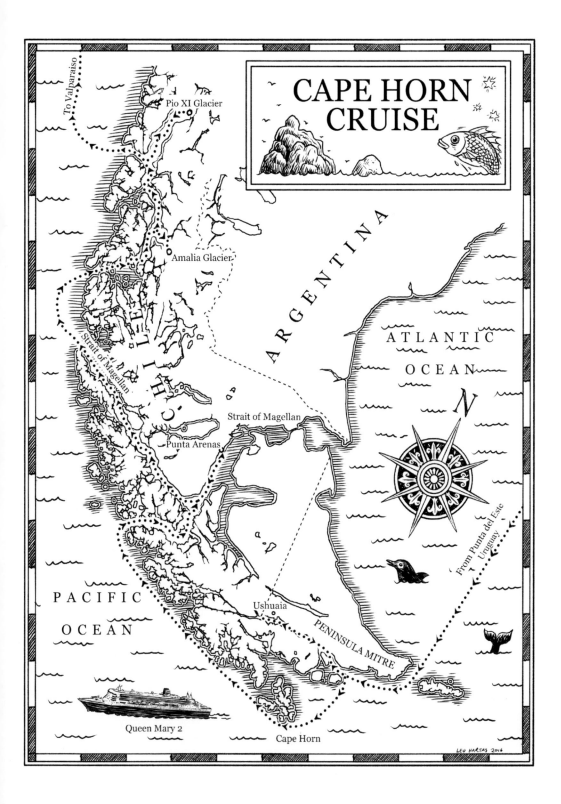

CAPE HORN CRUISE

To Valparaiso

Pio XI Glacier

Amalia Glacier

ARGENTINA

ATLANTIC OCEAN

CHILE

Strait of Magellan

Strait of Magellan

Punta Arenas

Ushuaia

PENINSULA MITRE

PACIFIC OCEAN

Queen Mary 2

Cape Horn

From Punta del Este Uruguay

LEO HARTAS 2016

Chapter One

Ranch

A group of about 50 of us flew from London to Rio de Janeiro on the first night of February to join the *Queen Mary 2* on her 2016 world voyage. The ship had taken 21 days to sail from Southampton to Rio de Janeiro, via New York, Fort Lauderdale and the Caribbean. The warm breath of the tropics greeted our arrival as we left the terminal after the 12-hour flight. It was nearly midnight, and, at 29C, still hotter than an English summer's day.

The Brazilian Cunard agents met us with cheery greetings and took us in coaches to a downtown hotel where we spent the night in air-conditioned comfort. In the morning we joined 1,300 passengers waiting to board the ship. At the same time an equal number were disembarking at the end of their cruise, about half of the ship's capacity of 2,620 guests.

Several coaches took us to the docks, ploughing their way through chaotic traffic. As we left the bus for the terminal, the resting *QM2* loomed over us, a huge grey mass brooding in the heatwaves. At check-in, a mug-shot is taken of each passenger which is digitally embedded in the passenger's all-important guest card. It is the key to your cabin (called a stateroom) and is used to identify passengers when leaving or re-boarding the ship at ports of call. The guest's picture comes up on a screen when the security person swipes the card. In the cashless environment on board, the card is used for all purchases including drinks. The bill is then charged to your credit card.

After the formalities it was an excellent moment stepping into my cabin, with the balcony overlooking the roofs and towers of Rio de Janeiro, with blue mountains beyond. I had a view of their poor answer to Table Mountain – Cape Town's iconic flat-topped guardian at the tip of Africa where, only five weeks earlier, I had spent the Christmas holidays. Here from the balcony of my cabin I could view a blue, shapeless ridge, punctuated by a peak, Corcovado, on which stands the giant statue of Christ the Redeemer.

When booking the cruise a year earlier I had chosen this particular cabin,12003, because it was on the highest deck, furthest forward and on the landward side. It was also near the inside cabin 12011 (which has no outer view) in which I had cruised to Cape Town in 2012. I wanted to be on the starboard side facing the land as we travelled south so that if coast was to be seen I would be on the more interesting side. I also chose a cabin as far forward as possible, the second from the front, with the tongue-in-cheek idea I would be one of the first to see anything.

Unfortunately, I had not taken into account that the bridge, from where the ship is driven and navigated, sits right across the width of the vessel just in front of, and at the same level, as the 12th deck cabins where I was. So though I was about 13 storeys above the waterline, the forward view was obscured. From my balcony looking forward I could see the chart screens glowing on the bridge through its rear windows. But with a wide view sideways and aft, this would be a minor inconvenience as the snowy mountains of Tierra del Fuego hove into view.

After two days' and three nights' sailing we reached Montevideo, capital of Uruguay in the broad estuary of the River Plate, and on about the same latitude as Cape Town. We were still in the hot zone of the southern summer. Whereas Africa ends in these latitudes at the Cape of Good Hope, South America goes on for another 1,300 miles south, curling into the frozen wastes at the ends of the earth.

Cruise ships usually arrive in the early morning and sail in the evening after passengers have had a jolly day in port. I was up at 5am, and, thanks to being on the right side of the ship, watched the dawn run-in past the land lights into the bay of Montevideo. The sun rising in the east was behind the city so all was rather silhouetted and indistinct.

The ship came in slowly through a narrow entrance, past a cluster of grey naval vessels moored to one side. I could see an officer on the *QM2* bridge moving quickly and intently from a chart screen to the wing of the bridge to have a look and back again to the monitor, like an airline pilot "landing" the craft. The ship entered a basin and made an amazing rotation on its axis in the confined space so that it could tie up at the dock facing the right way to depart in the evening.

I had signed up on the internet at home for a tour out of Montevideo called "A Day in the Countryside". As instructed we gathered in the Golden Lion pub at 8.30am and our group went down to the gangway on Deck 1 and boarded the buses, two for our tour. I had a South African sit down next to me; he boarded late and there were no more seats together so his wife sat elsewhere.

It turned out he lives in Four Ways, Sandton, outside Johannesburg, in the suburb of Lone Hill, near where Susan and I started married life in 1971 and had our firstborn, and also where later my Uncle Eric lived. George was good company for a chat both to and from the countryside and I met his wife during the excursion. We also had lunch together. Linda is from Essex, so if my English wife had been with me they could have exchanged notes about South African husbands and how difficult they can be.

Our coach stopped at two places in the city to let us get out and look around. One was a square with a statue of a Uruguayan hero, the other the legislative building, an elaborate baroque pile guarded by full-dress soldiers in the intense heat. The guide provided a commentary on Uruguay for the full 40 miles to the ranch and proved to be intensely proud and protective of her nation's reputation.

As we arrived at the ranch, or *estancia*, the look of the place made a fine first impression. Thousands of trees introduced by former custodians formed a wonderful parklike atmosphere with belts of acacia, oak, eucalyptus and other trees lining the fields. The land was lushly green, fed by water pumped from underground aquifers.

We were met by *gauchos*, cowboys and cowgirls on horseback holding Uruguayan flags in a salute of welcome. They trotted ahead of the coaches as we pulled into the yard, all beautifully shaded with a canopy of acacias. First came a welcoming drink. The guide had said on the coach that we would be offered beer, wine, fruit juice or water, and I thought uh-oh I don't have any currency, I'll have to go to the tap in the washrooms. But we were treated like visiting friends rather than customers. Complimentary beer and wine flowed from big bottles. After that we boarded trailers with hay bales for seats and some of the party volunteered to go in a horse and cart and a vintage truck.

I unwisely chose to sit in the front of a trailer so I had to eat dust from the rear wheels of the lorry. We toured the property, seeing dozens of horses in excellent condition, crops of soya and herds of dairy cattle. It is primarily a dairy farm, called La Rábida after a monastery near where the farm's founding family lived in Spain.

We got off the wagons at the seaside at a beach with millions of tiny shells washed up in banks of white. The ranch sometimes exercises its horses on the beach, letting them gallop through the shallows in clouds of spray, but not today. The water of this 137-mile-wide estuary of the River Plate, fed by the rivers Parana and Uruguay, was brown and muddy. "Plate" is an anglicisation of *Rio del la Plata*, *plata* being Spanish for silver.

After another dusty drive we returned to the yard of the homestead and the lady of the ranch told us about the underground water supply they rely on. She showed us a map of the extent of the aquifer reaching north into Brazil, and said that they have six boreholes which can produce 3,000 gallons a day each. There was a row of taps over a trough and we were all given our own glass to sample the waters.

Then on to lunch in a large area shaded by spreading acacias and in a low barn where we sat on more bales of hay. The family once had a big wedding there after converting the barn for the purpose. It was so successful that they decided to use the facility for visiting groups like ours. Any organisation wanting to show visitors the true glories of the Uruguayan *pampas* can bring their guests for the kind of experience we had.

Feast: *Roast lunch was already on the barbecue when we arrived at the La Rábida ranch in Uruguay.*

Picnic: *Guests gather for a picnic under the spreading acacias after touring the ranch.*

Meadow: *Equine contentment in the glossy fields of high summer at La Rábida.*

Starter: *Best bits from the barbecue go with drinks before the sit-down lunch.*

When we arrived the barbecue was well under way. It is called an *asado* in Spanish (the actual grill is called a *parrilla*). In South Africa we call it a *braai* (Dutch). For a Hispanic barbecue, the wood is burned in a separate brazier to make coals which are then transferred as needed with a spade to beneath the grids holding the meat. This contrasts with the method elsewhere of lighting a fire to make coals, then almost immediately starting to grill the meat when the fire is still too hot. The Spanish are not in a hurry as we are. Their way results in a slower, controlled and more even grilling. On this occasion we had pork, beef, sausage and chicken.

We were offered more beer and wine and for the starter were served sausage cut in rounds with roasted pieces of red and green sweet peppers and pumpkin. Helping ourselves, we skewered meat and veg on a cocktail stick and had the food as a canape with our beer and wine. The main course, for which we sat in the barn, consisted of the barbecued meat carved and served with roast potatoes, and a separate cold plate for salad. Our hosts could not do enough for us.

La Rábida belongs to the Artagaveytia-Pardo Santayanas family. The *grande dame* owner of the ranch who showed us around is a widow with six children, 16 grandchildren and so far two great grandchildren. Three daughters helped serve us food and drink.

Before dessert, a lovely gentle Jersey cow was brought and tied to a tree and the *gaucho* proceeded to demonstrate milking. Guests were invited to try pulling the teats. Later, when everyone had become used to the idea and liked their drink with cream, squirts of milk straight from the udder were put into people's coffee. Others put a glass under the teat and enjoyed the milk warm.

Unusually, I was brought up on milk warm from the cow. As a child on an African farm we had a glass of it, full cream of course, for supper just after milking time. All we did for hygiene was sieve it through a muslin cloth to remove specks of dust. Yet now I was not among those to step forward for milk straight from the cow. I realised I had come full circle and was now a squeamish townie.

Dessert was handed round during the time people were taking milk from the cow, and also on offer was a chance to have a bumpy ride on a cow-hide pulled on the grass behind a galloping horse. After that we all went off to the coaches with thanks and fond farewells and set off for our return to the ship. The guide advised us to have a *siesta* on the way, but George and I had another chat. He is a lifelong artist and showed me photos on his phone of his paintings.

We were soon back at the dock. I had a short wander into the streets nearby and had a look at two wartime naval prizes on display at the entrance to the harbour – the huge anchor of German warship the *Admiral Graf Spee*, as well as the rangefinder, used to line up her guns on the target. These are the only relics of the first important naval engagement of the Second World War, fought in 1939 in these remote waters, far from Europe on the River Plate, where the countries were neutral.

The pocket battleship *Admiral Graf Spee*, the most advanced warship of her type, had been sinking British merchant ships at will in the South Atlantic, reaching a tally of 19. Three Royal Navy cruisers caught up with the raider and the *Graf Spee* sustained crippling damage. Rather than surrender, the Germans fled to the neutral waters of the River Plate and scuttled *Graf Spee* (blew her up) just outside Montevideo Bay. Of course in Montevideo the exciting naval battles and the mighty explosion that sank the ship were sensations at the time and probably put the city firmly on the world map.

Back on board after our day in the countryside, the QM2 cast off while we were having dinner and slipped out of the harbour, bound for Punta del Este, a resort city and playground of the wealthy only about 100 miles east along the coast, and still in Uruguay. This "Cannes of South America", was originally to have been our only port of call in Uruguay, but at a late stage a berth became available for a stop in Montevideo too.

This was just as well.

Chapter Two

Companions

Cruise sceptics, and I was one once, find it hard to imagine life on board a liner. They suspect it will be dull, the same each day and not enough to do as you look out on the watery wastes. There may be a risk of it being dull, but there is certainly enough on offer; perhaps even too much to choose from.

When you wake up to a new day on the ocean, just like at home you can have tea or coffee in bed, or indeed, breakfast; a steward will bring it to you on a silver tray. Otherwise there is a spread in the buffet, the King's Court, on Deck 7 from 6.30am to 11.30am. Or if you want to socialise and be served at table, there is the Britannia restaurant on Deck 2 from 8am to 9.30am. A couple I met made it work by having the husband go to the buffet so his wife had the cabin to herself to complete her morning ablutions. Then they both went to the restaurant and the husband kept her company with a bowl of fruit.

At the restaurant, guests arriving at the head steward's stand are asked whether they are happy to join a group, and most agree. They are shown to a table where the other guests have just arrived so they are all at the same stage of ordering and having the meal served. It is a way of meeting people that puts you on your toes. There is always something new to be learned from strangers and their way of life.

My breakfast encounters included the sisters from Maine who travel the world taking wildlife photographs that they sell online; the retired lawyer from Alberta with stories of politics on the prairie; the couple from New Zealand who advised me to which archive I should send my grandfather's diaries of his visit there in 1937; and the people from Cumbria who suffered in the floods that hit northern England.

Dinnertime is different. There are two sittings, at 6pm and 8.30pm. You choose which time you want when you book your cruise. Your choice has implications for the way you spend each evening, because the nightly variety show in the Royal Court Theatre, *Showtime*, has an 8.45pm slot for the 6pm diners and a 10.30pm repeat for those who eat at 8.30. It is a choice of being either an early bird or a night owl.

If you dine at 6pm you finish in comfortable time to get a seat for the first show, which lasts about an hour. This allows you to go straight to the ballroom to catch the live band striking up at 9.45. If you are a keen dancer and want to skip the show there is "recorded strict tempo music" in the ballroom, the Queen's Room, from 8.30pm until the live band starts.

The night owl 8.30pm diners would go to the second variety show at 10.30 and join the dancers in the ballroom after that. Dancing continues in both the ballroom and the adjoining nightclub, which has a separate more jazzy live band, until well after midnight. On formal nights people dress up and the Queen's Room is decorated – in the case of our cruise – for the "Black and White Ball", the "Carnival Ball", the "Valentine's Ball" and the "Starlight Ball", during which there are also floor shows by professional dancers.

For dinner, which kicks off your super sociable evening with multiple fine-dining menu choices and an attentive wine steward, you are seated with the same people each night. This works well and you make friendships that remain in your thoughts for a long time. The enforced familiarity produces entertaining conversation, banter, good humour, and serious topics, either in the round or one on one.

We had a corner table at sea level, end-on to the tossing waves that reel past the window. We should have had eight people but one chair remained empty for a mystery guest. There was only one couple, Ray and Dot, from New

Jersey, and the rest of us were travelling alone. Ray is a retired insurance executive, full of good sense and tales of travel. Dot was a quiet, dignified presence who didn't often speak across the table. Except for sounding me out about the safety of a holiday in Cape Town, we didn't say much to one another.

Next to them usually sat Marc, from Fort Lauderdale, who worked for Ted Turner, the US cable television mogul. He is a great fan of Cunard and a student of the finest details of its ships. He was going on the full circumnavigation world cruise.

So was Gladys, a handsome, twice widowed Chilean-American from Washington D.C. Her first husband was an American diplomat and her second a financier. I usually sat beside her and was entertained with stories of a crowded life filled with travel and family. She was on friendly terms with another single traveller, Marie, from Sydney, Australia, who, like Gladys, was always carefully dressed and sure-footed in social situations. Marie was the only one of us still working, but able to take extended holidays because of her job's long-service entitlements.

Nelly often sat on my right with the empty chair beside her, so I did my best to include her in conversation. She is a Bulgarian-British accountant living in London. After the cruise she sent round by email a delightful picture of our table that she had asked the steward to take on her camera. The email's subject line was the very appropriate "Hello from Queen Merry table".

And as for me, in man heaven without wifely responsibilities, I certainly had a merry time, enjoying the choice of dining and food, chatting to people in the bar, and being diligent about exercise on the decks and stairs. In my cabin I devoured the view from my balcony with binoculars while following the navigation of the ship – where we were and where we were going – and paying attention to technical details, such as visiting the area where guests can view the ship's officers at work on the bridge.

While I had no trouble occupying my time with things that interested me, it is true that a cruise for all its novelty and comfort puts you in a rather artificial, limited-dimension environment. Comparing it with life at home, you realise that normality has a richer tapestry with its home management, family and social interactions and even the minor daily annoyances. Nevertheless, I kept in mind this is a holiday from it all and normal life can wait.

What I didn't realise is that I could have made it better. I discovered rather late in the voyage that like most things in life you have to get out there and make an effort in order to reap the rewards. At breakfast one morning towards the end of the cruise I was seated opposite Diana, a guest from Cheshire who I met briefly at the Captain's cocktail party. She picked up from a remark I made that I was perhaps getting tired of life on board. She asked me what activities I had taken up and I told her not any really.

She said she had joined a "Bridge for Beginners" class that met every day, taught by a Canadian couple. She had known nothing of the card game and had enjoyed the instruction enough to look forward to it each day. The same went for dancing. There were line dancing classes every morning and ballroom classes in the afternoon, with ample opportunity to practise steps all night long when taped or live music played in the ballroom. No, I had not signed up for any of that because, I explained weakly, it would have been a bit of a stretch.

This was a lightbulb moment. I realised that getting out of the comfort zone is what a cruise, or any holiday, should be about. Thinking about it, I am sure I would have enjoyed learning bridge. A friend of the family had taught me as a teenager but I had never played again. And dancing? Well, so what if I made a fool of myself, I would not see the people again. In fact I could have been Mr Anonymous and danced a mangled tango with a stem in my mouth for all they cared. I then regretted missing one-time opportunities that were free for the taking in the safe environment of the ship.

Our dinner companion Marie was a keen dancer, going to classes in the day, as did Gladys and Nelly, and also Diana. As singles this may have been one of their main reasons for going on a cruise, and they were not alone. There were said to be about 150 single women guests on board of whom about 120 were dance enthusiasts. From being in the ballroom in the evenings I got to know many of them by sight – serious faces sitting alone or in groups around the edge of the dance floor; not showing much joy but excellent on their feet when dancing.

"Welcome to Queen Merry table" – nightly dining companions left to right: Nelly, author, Gladys, Ray, Dot, Marc, and Marie.

(Photo credit: Cunard steward)

The author on the top deck at one of two glaciers visited by QM2 in the fjords of southern Chile; the Pio XI glacier.

Cunard provides "gentlemen dancers" to pair off with the single guests. I was told there are about 80 of them who get board and accommodation but no pay for the cruise. These lucky gents range from young to old and there is keen competition among the single women for their attentions on the dance floor.

Marie would complain that if she were to sit on one side of the ballroom, the gentlemen would be all on the other side asking the single women that side to dance. If she moved across in the hope of being noticed, there was still no guarantee she would be asked. It was all rather tiresome to have to wait on a whim.

It reminded me of Jane Austen's era with its strict social graces, when the "wallflowers" waited and hoped that a man, any man, would ask them for the next dance. I composed some advice for solo travellers: *"It is a truth universally acknowledged, that a single man . . . seeking friendship on a Cunard cruise, should know how to dance"*.[1]

On the second night of the cruise, hearing that Marie was going straight to the ballroom after dinner, I rashly offered to go with her to have a go at the dancing. When we got there, she was obviously in her element and in familiar territory, which I was not. She made a beeline for a place at the front, on the edge of the dance floor and we paused to take in the scene.

A tune was playing that I thought I could manage so we got to our feet. Of course you need to wait for the correct moment in the rhythm to take the first step, but I got off on the wrong foot. Our dance was brief; my quickstep was out of time and my waltz wasn't working. I used to dance quite rhythmically and knew the basic steps but was now out of practice and lacked confidence. I realised Marie is a serious dancer and I am not. Yet if I had taken my "Jane Austen advice", I could have started dance classes the next day with the full cruise ahead of me.

While the prominence of shipboard dancing was new to me, there are many other fulfilling activities. The *Daily Programme* for the next day is laid out with the pillow chocolates on your turned-down bed when you get back to

---

1   With apologies to Jane Austen's famous opening line of *Pride and Prejudice*.

your cabin each evening. It describes events and happenings hour by hour from 6am to midnight.

This is a typical list *(you will be tested on this)*: fitness sessions in the gym, fencing, Christian fellowship, bridge lessons, line dancing, ballroom dancing, hairstyling lessons, water colour painting, lectures on sea creatures, knitting and sewing, jewellery making, history lectures *(keep up there at the back!)*, scarf tying, planetarium shows, deck quoits, introduction to acupuncture, Skype seminar *(are you still with me?)*, Texas hold 'em Tournament, movies *(Max, Bridge of Spies)*, Trivial Pursuit in the pub, and Getting to Know your iPad.

If variety was the ambition it was surprising that Cunard did not make more of the fact that we were visiting a cardinal point on the globe. Celebration of the geography of our cruise was almost completely absent, although we did get a commemorative certificate for rounding the Horn. From talking to other guests I was surprised how many shared my interest in just being able to go to the Cape and see it. Yet there was no build-up, and our curiosity about our surroundings went unfed by lecture or bulletin.

When we were at Tierra del Fuego there was a stampede to the ship's library to look at the atlases and study the route. But the atlases had maps only of the whole of South America with the Cape Horn bit too small in scale to see much. I had with me two large-scale detailed charts of the Cape Horn area I bought at Stanfords, the famous London map shop, so I presented one of them to the grateful librarian.

The *QM2* boasts the only Planetarium afloat. I thought this meant one could study the actual stars overhead during the voyage, but it is only another form of movie, similar to Imax. Virtual star-gazing is held in a theatre called Illuminations where films are shown and talks presented. There is a white circular screen on the ceiling and a section of seats in the middle of the theatre where the chairs tilt back so you can look up at the ceiling. From four glass domes positioned in a square round the seating area, they project wonderful 3D images of the night sky.

A voice-over explains the solar system and how all matter is governed by the chemistry and physics of the universe. The materials that make up our bodies come from the stars. *So here we are.* Maybe when our prehistoric forebears gazed up at the infinite revolving pinpricks in the night sky and wondered what they were, they invented spiritual beings and gave them a home in the heavens, just to make some sense of their human existence.

Now we make sense of it with parties on a ship.

Chapter Three

Tierra del Fuego

After leaving hot and sunny Uruguay on Saturday 6 February, we had three days at sea heading for Tierra del Fuego and Cape Horn. Each day the skies became greyer and cloudier, and the tropical vibe gradually faded as the winds freshened and the sea and air temperatures became colder. By Monday, we were far south off the coast of Patagonia with the Falkland Islands nearby and 600 miles to go to the end of South America. The daily log of the voyage that is posted on a noticeboard each day reported that at noon the sea temperature was only 10C and the air 14C. Welcome to the austral summer.

The next day was Shrove Tuesday, when Christians mark the last day before the beginning of Lent by making pancakes so that luxury ingredients like butter, flour and milk are used up before fasting (or at least cutting back) until Easter. The change in the tempo of the cruise was marked by the traditional pancake races having to be moved from the open decks to the ballroom because of high winds. The gale was Force 8, defined on the Beaufort Scale as a "fresh" wind, with moderately high waves breaking white at the crests.

That night as we sailed past the eastern extremity of Tierra del Fuego, the Mitre Peninsula, which looks more like the tip of a horn than Cape Horn itself, the wind grew stronger. It came from the south-west, the classic direction from which Cape Horn's storms are brewed. Our westward course was taking the *QM2* straight into the teeth of it.

In the warmth and light of my cabin there was a low whistling noise outside the glass door to my balcony. I went out to look but could hardly open and shut the door. Back inside, the sound of the wind was punctuated by low booming sounds far away, as if the hull of the ship was punching its way through a moveable force. The *QM2* gently pitched and heeled without any sudden or violent motion. Beneath my feet the floor fell away slightly and suddenly tipped, then righted itself, as if regaining its poise.

The ship was basically stable but perhaps having to deal with the onslaught of the odd rogue wave. For a proper sailor this would have been small beer but for me quite thrilling. What were those booming noises? Was it the mighty battle between the mongoose wind and the cobra sea? With the unflinching power of the ship vanquishing them both? But after a while I wished the fierce rushing sound of the wind would go away as it sometimes reached a pitch that quite bothered me.

I thought of the thousands of sailors in this weather in laughably small ships, depending on ropes, canvas and a wooden rudder moved only by muscle power. Unlike power-driven ships they had to avoid facing up to a strong gale bearing down on them head on. If they tried to ride it out with the sharp end to the wind the ship might be swept backwards and lose the ability to steer. The gusts could carry away the masts and rigging, leaving them at the mercy of wind and current. One of the solutions was to "wear" the ship, turn it away and zig-zag with the wind coming from one side or the other, while still trying to keep on course.

Captain James Cook the British explorer and navigator who did more than anyone to spearhead maritime and geographic knowledge of the Pacific and southern oceans, sailed from Rio de Janeiro to Cape Horn in the summer of 1769 aboard the *Endeavour*. In his *Journals*, he relates how he was caught in a gale (probably to him unexceptional) similar to the weather we experienced in roughly the same place:

[2]**Saturday 7th January** *First part Strong gales with excessive hard Squales [squalls] accompney'd with rain, at 9pm wore and brought too her head to the westward under Main sail, and reef'd the Fore sail for the*

---

2   The Hakluyt Society, the publisher of scholarly editions of voyages and travels, retains Cook's idiosyncratic spelling.

*first time; the Storm continued with little intermission untill toward Noon
when it abated so as we could set the Topsails close reef'd.*

Cook and his crew would have been calmly out there in the raw wind and
sea, lit only by lanterns swinging on their hooks, working with the weather
to keep afloat and navigate the ship, not hiding behind the curtains or
dancing in the ballroom as we were. I happened to be reading Samuel
Johnson's *A Journey to the Western Islands of Scotland* (1773), an arduous
tour that occurred at the same time as Cook's voyages. The Hebrides in
those days sounded just as wild and uncongenial as Cape Horn.

While we slept through the storm, the *QM2* stopped, or at least slowed
down, to pick up, near the mouth of the Beagle Channel, a pilot who
knew these waters. He was to guide us in the darkness westward towards
Ushuaia, Argentina. The master, Captain Kevin Oprey, had told us at noon
in his daily navigational announcement that we would reach the Beagle
Channel in the night and have a local pilot on board thereafter until we left
the area of Cape Horn five days later. Oprey added that he as master was
prepared to be on the bridge night and day to ensure the safety of the ship.

In the morning as dawn broke we sailed slowly up to the port of Ushuaia,
which I later found the locals pronounce *Oos-why-a*. It was one of the
occasions where my choice of vantage point in the ship paid off. On getting
out of bed I drew the curtains back and there was the payback moment.
Facing the land I could watch the searchlight sun beaming itself on to the
shore as it rose behind the ship, gradually rolling back the ghostly mountain
shadows and dawn twilight.

Except for town buildings, the coastline was covered with thick vegetation
rising up to the base of the mountains. Peaks ranged inland in high
procession, one after the other, crowned with eternal snow and wreathed
in swirling mist like the "cloud capp'd towers" of Shakespeare's *Tempest*.

The dawn spectacle as the ship moved slowly to her anchorage presented
a magnificent evolving scene that dwarfed the town and must have been
gazed upon in wonder by centuries of intrepid sailors. It was our first
landfall after leaving Uruguay. South America's southern extremity could
not have made a more dramatic first impression.

Towers: *The wild shoreline of Tierra del Fuego as* QM2 *approaches the port of Ushuaia in Argentina.*

Sunrise: *Magical dawn as we make first landfall after our voyage from the hot zone of the South American summer.*

Pristine: *The unsullied scene that greeted us at the start of the Tierra Major Nature Reserve Trek on Tierra del Fuego.*

Trek: *Walkers from QM2 toil up a slope towards the glacier viewpoint on the nature reserve hike.*

The announcement from the bridge of our arrival said that the wind was still too fresh to swing out the tenders – the lifeboats used to ferry passengers ashore – and get them ready for their task. But not long after, the wind dropped and it was time to assemble for our shore excursions.

I signed up for a hike called the "Tierra Major Nature Reserve Trek" so that I could experience the famous Tierra del Fuego with boots on the ground. The name means Land of Fire. It is by far the largest island of the Cape Horn archipelago, about the size of Ireland. Two-thirds of it belongs to Chile and the rest to Argentina.

To the north it forms the southern shore of the Magellan Strait. When the strait was discovered by Ferdinand Magellan in 1520 he was the first to see many fires on shore and named it Tierra del Fuego. Later it was discovered the flames were the campfires of the native inhabitants keeping warm. These people, now unfortunately extinct but memorialised in the museums of Ushuaia and Punta Arenas in Chile, lived a precarious hunter-gatherer existence with the most rudimentary forms of clothing and shelter.

On shore we were greeted by a sign that said "Welcome to the End of the World" *(Fin del Mundo)*. Ushuaia claims to be the most southerly settlement in the world but this ignores the existence of Puerto Williams across the Beagle Channel on the Chilean side. They may be remote, yet these places have all modern conveniences and a thriving commerce based on tourism and cruise ships, from taxi services to boat trips and even rail tours.

Ushuaia is the main supply base and jumping off point for visits to Antarctica, 600 miles to the south across the Drake Passage. A ship was in port that takes passengers to the island that forms Cape Horn, *Isla Hornos*, where visitors can clamber ashore up a steep cliff and say they have actually stood at the Cape.

A party of about 35 of us set off in a coach with an English-speaking local guide to enjoy a day close to nature on Tierra del Fuego. We took the main highway north-east out of town through the steep and spectacular Olivia River Valley. National Route 3 is an Argentinian main road interrupted at the Chilean border at a place on the east coast of Tierra del Fuego called San Sebastián. There you have to take a road through Chile that crosses the Strait of Magellan by ferry at Punta Delgada. Soon after, you cross the border again to re-enter Argentina and resume your journey on National Route 3.

It must be a nuisance to Argentinians not to have a direct land route between their most southerly city and that part of their country they call the Continent – mainland South America. As can be imagined there was bitter disagreement in setting the national boundary in these parts. A compromise on the boundary was arbitrated by the British in 1902.

Our coach stopped nowhere in particular on the side of the highway beside a colourful clump of lupins. Down a short path we came to a wooden hut called a *nunatak* where we were invited to change our footwear for rubber boots. I was not keen as I had brought my bulky hiking boots all the way from England, but the guide assured me it would be very muddy and I would need the rubber.

And so it proved. There was a lot of squelching through clumps of grass along the boggy paths. As you stepped on the peat it would release water underfoot like a sponge. I was also glad to leave my jersey behind in the hut. I was expecting a bleak, infertile countryside with cold winds and maybe showers of rain, so wore a raincoat with a layer underneath. Not only was the jersey redundant but the raincoat too. Instead, I needed a sun hat.

After most of us had been helped to find the right size boots we set off in double file with three guides – some of them assigned to help the less stable of us over rough ground. The immediate impression was spectacular: a lush green valley, soft underfoot, adorned with trees and flowering shrubs; a clean, fresh, bracing environment, the air crisp and unsullied. Unlike the cordillera of North America, in these latitudes the most common indigenous mountain tree is the deciduous beech with its cute little green leaves, rather than the conifer which is ubiquitous to Canada and Siberia.

They tried to introduce the Canadian beaver to these parts as a commercial activity, but it was not a success as there was no market, at least from this distance, for their furs. Instead beaver dam building (they build lodges surrounded by water to keep safe from predators) inundated the landscape and killed off a lot of the trees on the valley bottom. We saw standing water and streams strewn with the grey skeletal remains of tree trunks and branches.

We visited a waterfall and came within view of the foot of a glacier, where we were offered tea and biscuits by the guides, before continuing our three-mile round trip through woods and meadows back to the wooden cabin. On the way we saw wildflowers, including little orchids, and I wondered whether any plants belonged to the same botanical families that grow at the Cape of South Africa. Quite possibly, billions of years ago when Earth was one continent, this part was hugging Cape Town, as the Horn does curve that way.

Back in the *nunatak* we had tea or coffee, sandwiches and apple cake, and retrieved our footwear before saying farewell to the guides, some of whom were now barbecuing meat for the next party of visitors. The coach retraced its route to Ushuaia past sheer cliffs of rock and mountain vistas and let us off in the harbour near the pier. There was a very long queue of people. It turned out to be returning passengers like ourselves waiting to board the tenders.

We lined up for an hour and there were many impatient passengers who took it out on the longsuffering Cunard officers supervising the boarding. It was said that the delay was the result of a dispute between the Argentinian harbour officials and Cunard. The officials had ordered the tenders to fly the Argentinian national flag but Cunard refused. The blue Argentinian flag was however flying at the *QM2* masthead as is customary for a visiting ship in port.

The gossip was that the Argentinians retaliated by reducing the available gangways from two to one for boarding the tenders, so the process of transferring to the ship took much longer. As we know from the Falkland Islands dispute, there is no love lost between the Argentinians and the British. While there were banners at the port protesting against British "occupation" of the Falklands, we were all hospitably treated by the friendly locals.

Just as could be expected.

Chapter Four

Horn

The evening we left Ushuaia heading south-east for Cape Horn was the polar opposite of the night of our arrival. The storm-tossed Beagle Channel of 24 hours before had become as still as a Scottish loch. The narrow waterway forms a boundary between Argentina on the north side and the Island of Navarino on the south side that belongs to Chile.

This sometimes quiet channel bears the name given to it on the first voyage of HMS *Beagle* in the 19th century. She was sent to conduct a hydrographic survey of Patagonia and Tierra del Fuego that took place between 1827 and 1829, surveying the coasts, sounding depths and filling in the blanks on navigational charts.

Charles Darwin was on board the *Beagle* for its second voyage in the early 1830s as gentleman companion to the captain, Robert FitzRoy. This was the voyage during which Darwin made the scientific discoveries which helped him formulate his theory of evolution (as opposed to divine creation). The voyage was also marked by the dropping off of supplies on the Island of Navarino for the establishment of a Christian mission station by the London Missionary Society. The mission did not succeed for long.

Back in the here and now, from my *QM2* balcony, with the sun setting behind the ship, I was able to look across to the romantic snowy mountains of Navarino on our starboard side and enjoy a scene of sublime quiet, completely at odds with the climatic and historical reputation of our destination.

That night our course took us back along the Beagle Channel the way we had come and then south to Cape Horn, making landfall at the outermost tip of South America in the dawn of the next day, 11 February. I was woken at 4.45am by a violent motion of the ship that tossed my body to one side. There was no more drama after that but I could not go back to sleep. Outside it was dark and the wind gusted and whistled against the balcony door.

As soon as it was light enough I dressed and went up to the Observation deck at the front of the ship just one level lower than my cabin. It was very blowy and I was surprised the decks were not shut off – they rope off the doors with a sign Closed High Wind when conditions are rough.

There was already quite a crowd, mainly Germans and Americans, in puffy coats and anoraks with hoods, peering through binoculars at the murky view. Bits of land could be seen ahead and to the right, but no one was sure what they were looking at. Was this the island of Cape Horn? It certainly looked the part. Most of us stood well back against the bulkhead to shelter from the cold wind and squalls of rain.

After a while the QM2 turned to starboard and we were told that a low strip of land now slipping away to our left was the actual Cape Horn. It was misty, windy and cold and quite dreary so I went below. After the break the weather improved. An announcement from the bridge said that the ship was doing an anti-clockwise circumnavigation of the island and then it would turn and do a clockwise rotation so we could see it from all angles.

I spent most of the morning viewing and photographing Cape Horn from the upper decks. The wind was cold but not too strong, and there were no rain showers. For Cape Horn it was probably a pretty good day. Earlier there was weak sun through the scudding clouds, then later the sun came out fully in a blue sky.

It was a seascape with island and rocks, some dangerously half-submerged with waves breaking white around them. Cape Horn and surrounding islands are bare of trees, just grass and rock, like the tops of mountains up to their necks in sea. The most prominent landmark is a peak 1,400ft high on one side of the island. James Cook in the Endeavour observed in January 1769 the same scenes we saw, except he had foggier weather. He wrote in his *Journal of the First Voyage* (1768-1771): *"It appeared not unlike an Island with a very high round hummock upon it: this I believe to be Cape Horn . . ."*

The other notable feature is a modern innovation, the Chilean naval station. Unlike the peak, it is best seen through binoculars as it looks so small from far off. It is located on the headland that forms the southern tip of the island. By the time of our clockwise circumnavigation it was possible to view this southernmost point quite clearly – a green breast of land in the sunshine, treeless but thickly grassed from the almost constant rainfall.

The Chileans have decided they need to keep a presence at the Horn, however remote it is. The authorities arrange for volunteer families to live at the naval station for periods of several months on a rotational basis so that there is always a citizen of Chile "in possession".

The naval station is grouped with a little lighthouse and a memorial to the many sailors who lost their lives rounding the Horn. It is said to be in the shape of an albatross, the giant seabird that was regarded by sailors as a good omen if it kept company with their ship. It has wings with the widest span of any bird as it soars on the wind currents. I looked at the memorial through binoculars and decided the shape of the albatross must be quite abstract. It was put up in 1992.

A map of historic landmarks in the Cape Horn area published in Argentina by Zagier & Urruty Publications[3] shows the extraordinary extent of shipwrecks in these waters. The actual loss of life can only be guessed at. The map, which I bought in London, depicts the location of only some of the wrecks, with ship names and symbols for different types of vessels from small sailing ships to steamers. There are 149 ships listed as having foundered between the year 1643 (presumably when records began) and 1990, of which 68, mainly smaller sailing craft, went down off Cape Horn.

The worst year was 1900 when no less than eight ships lost the battle against the combined forces of wind, wave and current. There is a cold water current that flows west-to-east round the Horn, speeded by the relative narrowing between the land masses of South America and the Antarctic Peninsula.

---

3   Cabo de Hornos, Isla de los Estados, Peninsula Mitre, Carta Historica, 2006.

This also quickens winds blowing in the same direction through the gap. The next most hazardous stretch of water surrounds the Mitre Peninsula and Staten Island to the north-east, where ships would have approached Cape Horn against the wind, as we did, through the De Le Maire Strait.

By lunch time I had seen enough of the waves and islands and went down to the comfort of the Britannia restaurant for lunch where, strangely, a discussion of our morning's leisure was not on the menu. We did have good weather for the legendary Horn so I suppose it was a case of good news is no news.

Soon after 3pm the *QM2* completed her visit and set off at a leisurely 17 knots (about 20mph) on a north-westerly course on the open ocean outside the groups of offshore islands. We were sailing for the Cockburn Channel, an opening in the islands that would take us to the mid-section of the Strait of Magellan and on to Punta Arenas in Chile.

Soon all that could be seen on the starboard side were far off land forms in the gathering rain and mist as the weather worsened. From my balcony I could peer at the coast where Cook, then Commander of the *Resolution*, called to take on food and water at Christmas 1774. According to his *Journal of the Second Voyage* (1772-1775), while his first impressions of the land were of mixed dismay and wonder, it turned out to be a bumper Christmas for him and his crew.

He wrote that the mountains presented the most desolate and barren aspect that he had ever seen.[4] ". . . *these Mountains terminate in horroable precipices whose craggy summits spire up to a vast height, so that hardly any thing in nature can appear with a more barren and savage aspect than the whole of this coast.*"

As barren as it was it was not without people. The natives visited Cook's ship and came on board the *Resolution* on Christmas Day, seeming to be well acquainted with Europeans.

---

4   The Hakluyt Society, the publisher of scholarly editions of voyages and travels, retains Cook's idiosyncratic spelling.

Quiet: *The QM2 glides down the Beagle Channel bound for Cape Horn after leaving Ushuaia, 10 February.*

Ahoy: *View at first light of Cape Horn, the tip of land to the left, from the Observation deck, 11 February.*

Lookout: *The 1,400ft peak on the island of Cape Horn seen as the weather improves during our second circumnavigation.*

Rush hour: *While the QM2 was at Cape Horn, another cruise ship the* Stella Australis *was discharging passengers who climbed the cliffs to visit the Chilean naval station (centre on ridge).*

"*They were almost Naked; their cloathing was a Seal skin, some had two or three sew'd together, so as to make a cloak which reach'd to the knee, but most of them had only one skin hardly large enough to cover their shoulders, and all their lower parts were quite naked.* [The women and children] *remained in the Canoes. I saw two young Children at the breast, as naked as they were born; thus they are inured from their infancy to Cold and hardships.*"

In each canoe was a fire over which they huddled to keep warm. "*I cannot suppose that they carry a fire in their Canoes for this purpose only, but rather that it may be allways ready to remove a shore wherever they land; for let their method of obtaining fire be what it will, they cannot be allways sure of finding dry fuel that will take fire from a spark.*"

The previous day, Christmas Eve, in fine pleasant weather, Cook's party had shot 62 geese on which they feasted. Cook wrote that the natives "*did not wait to pertake of our Christmas Cheer. . . we had not experienced such fare for some time, Roast and boiled Geese, Goose pies &c was victuals little known to us, and we had yet some Madeira Wine left, which was the only Article of our provisions that was mended by keeping; so that our friends in England did not perhaps, celebrate Christmas more cheerfully than we did.*" Appropriately he gave his anchorage the name Christmas Sound.

On the *QM2* during the night another Force 9 gale erupted and I could hear and feel the forces at work on the open sea. At some point we turned north-east to negotiate the Cockburn Channel where in the shelter of the islands the weather calmed down. By dawn we were arriving serenely at Punta Arenas, the main port on the famous Magellan Strait.

Ferdinand Magellan was a Portuguese navigator in the service of the King of Spain. He had been knocking on the door of the South American east coast for a year, investigating every opening and inlet for a channel that would lead westward. His purpose was to win Spain an advantage over the Portuguese monopoly of trade to the east round Africa by finding a route westward to the Spice Islands. He thought he had found it at the River Plate but was sorely disappointed.

But on 21 October 1520, lookouts on his fleet of four ships sighted a promontory, beyond which stretched an expanse of dark water to the west. Two ships were sent to investigate. They came back with the stunning news that it was saltwater as far as they had sailed in five days. Casting their leads for depth they could not touch bottom, and tides ebbed and flowed on the shores.

They had, sensationally, found the mouth of the supposed but never proven passage west through the continental barrier. Though the strait proved to be a complicated maze, after a month Magellan burst upon the sea that came to be known as the Pacific Ocean, the first European to do so. He also burst into tears with relief. Nearly 60 years later in 1578, Sir Francis Drake was the first Englishman to pass through the strait, with the much darker purpose of plundering Spain's west coast possessions.

Punta Arenas is all about Magellan: even the university is named after him, so I took the Cunard excursion, "Magellan's Discovery". The shady main square of the city has a fine statue of Magellan entitled *Hernando de Magallanes* overlooked by the Cape Horn Hotel and the Cathedral. But of greater interest was the open-air museum out of town where there are replicas of Magellan's flagship *Nao Victoria* (*nao* means "big ship", or carrack) and HMS *Beagle*, both built in a labour of love by Chilean enthusiasts from local timber.

Construction of the replica HMS *Beagle* started in 2012 and the interior of the ship was still being fitted out when we visited. Darwin complained of the "want of room" inside her. As I explored her lower decks I could see why; it was rather tight for 65 crewmen and stores for several years' occupation.

Magellan's ship, built 300 years earlier than the original *Beagle*, would have been even more uncomfortable for its crew of about 40. I paced out the length of the *Victoria*. It is only 65ft which means that two of the ships of Magellan's fleet could comfortably have fitted in the *QM2*'s dining room. I walked the decks of the 85-ton replica and went below to see the sleeping quarters where a hammock is slung in a space too low to kneel upright. I explored the lower storage decks, and the relatively roomy captain's cabin housed in the towering aftcastle.

Thoughts turned again to the hardships of being on board vessels like these in the Cape Horn, or any, climate – sharing small spaces in rotation with sea-going duties and being pitched about in perilous seas, with an uncertain destination and voyages measured in years.

An American on the bus back to the *QM2*, using a starkly modern concept, remarked that the navigators must have had "a great commitment to exploration". But it was more than that. In those 16th century days the *Victoria* would have been the ultimate in transport technology, its purpose the noble trade in pepper and spices from the East to Europe, which would have been the greatest commercial prize of the time. Spices created fortunes, as oil did in our time.

Having found the legendary *paso*, the Spanish tried to secure their monopoly of trade to the West. They built two forts on the strait to stop English and Dutch competitors from sailing through. The forts were a failure. On these bleak and wintry shores the garrisons died horribly from want of food and supplies. One site, near Punta Arenas, came to be called Port Famine.

In an unconcious but nevertheless unworthy show of disrespect towards the nightmare hardships of our forebears at sea, back on board the *QM2* I had a beef and mushroom pie in the Golden Lion pub, and later relaxed on deck in the sunshine with a glass of champagne, listening to the jazz band playing "sailaway music" as we left Punta Arenas.

Port Famine it was not.

Storm: *A gale whips the sea and masks the distant coast near Cape Horn. Behind the mountains Commander James Cook and his crew spent Christmas 1774.*

Heroic: *A replica of Ferdinand Magellan's ship* Victoria *at a maritime museum outside Punta Arenas on the Magellan Strait, the passage he discovered in 1520.*

Dwarfed: *The replica of Magellan's ship in all its frailty, about 65ft in length and the height of just two decks of the QM2.*

Origin: *The replica of HMS* Beagle *at Punta Arenas made by local artisans to salute the ship that carried Charles Darwin, architect of the theory of evolution.*

Acknowledgements

The author acknowledges with thanks the use of quotations and references from the following publications.

Alan Moorehead, *Darwin and the Beagle*. Penguin Books, 1971. First published by Hamish Hamilton, 1969.

James Cook, *The Journals*. Penguin Classics, 2003. First published by The Hakluyt Society, 1955-1967 in four volumes.

William Manchester, *A World Lit only by Fire, The Medieval Mind and the Renaissance, Portrait of an Age*. Little, Brown and Company (Canada) Limited, 1992.

Hakluyt's Voyages, a Selection by Richard David. Chatto & Windus Ltd, 1981.

About the author

Hugh Leggatt was born in South Africa but has lived more than half his life in Canada and the United Kingdom. He started as a reporter on the Johannesburg *Star* before emigrating in 1980 to Vancouver with his wife and young family. After a short time with the Vancouver *Province*, he joined the mining industry where for 30 years he filled corporate communications and editorial roles for large global mining and metals companies including Rio Tinto plc in London.